# SAN FRANCISCO

## THE CITY AT A GLANCE

D0231868

**Transamerica Pyramid**
The most recognisable skyscraper i
it towers over the Financial District at 259m
tall. It's no longer home to the Transamerica
Corporation, but the name has stuck.
*See p013*

**City Hall**
The central building in the Civic Center, with
its gilded dome, was badly damaged in the
1989 earthquake. Renovation after 1995 saw
it returned to its former glory.
*See p065*

**Ferry Building**
Until the 1930s, this was the main arrival
point in the city. Today, it houses a vast
marketplace selling fresh local produce.
*The Embarcadero/Market Street*

**Market Street**
This thoroughfare runs diagonally from The
Castro to the Ferry Building, and is one of the
main routes for the renovated 1950s trams.

**San Francisco Museum of Modern Art**
One of the earliest 'destination' galleries, the
distinctive stripes and looming 'eye' of Mario
Botta's 1995 landmark are still impressive,
despite being dwarfed by newer buildings.
*See p036*

**Bay Bridge**
The busiest bridge in the US carries around
270,000 vehicles a day across the Bay to
Oakland and Berkeley.

# INTRODUCTION
## THE CHANGING FACE OF THE URBAN SCENE

Perhaps the most cosmopolitan of all US cities, San Francisco is not only blessed with a laid-back, liberal mindset, but also with a stunning, dramatic setting that only adds to its allure. Perched on a peninsula by a bay opening onto the Pacific Ocean, the agreeable (if unpredictable) climate and sea air are a rare treat in such a major metropolis. It's an enthralling city of contradictions, with traditional architecture and directional new buildings sitting side by side, 1950s trams sharing the streets with 21st-century hybrid cars, old-world museums next door to concept spaces, and a cheeriness in the locals that belies the knowledge that their home sits atop one of the world's more volatile fault lines.

Less daunting and aggressive than New York and more compact than Los Angeles, San Francisco is relatively straightforward to navigate (though, as in most US cities, it helps to have a car to get about). Couple this with the different cliques and tribes sticking to fairly defined neighbourhoods and you should be able to see the place from your preferred angle without too much trouble.

From the old-money mansions of Pacific Heights to the edgy creativity of The Mission and flamboyancy of The Castro, San Francisco is currently on a roll, and a resurgent economy after the dotbomb days has helped fuel a slew of prominent new builds by the likes of Herzog & de Meuron, Ricardo Legorreta and Morphosis, all of which have helped increase the city's global presence.

# ESSENTIAL INFO

## FACTS, FIGURES AND USEFUL ADDRESSES

### TOURIST OFFICE
Visitor Information Center
900 Market Street
T 888 782 9673
onlyinsanfrancisco.com

### TRANSPORT
**Car hire**
Avis
San Francisco International Airport
T 650 877 6780
www.avis.com
Hertz
433 Mason Street
T 415 771 2200
www.hertz.com
**Cable cars and trolleybuses**
Muni
www.sfmuni.com
**Taxis**
Luxor Cabs
T 415 282 4141
www.luxorcab.com
Yellow Cab Cooperative
T 415 626 2345
www.yellowcabsf.com

### EMERGENCY SERVICES
**Ambulance/Fire/Police**
T 911
**24-hour pharmacy**
Walgreens
459 Powell Street
T 415 984 0790
www.walgreens.com

### CONSULATE
**British Consulate-General**
Suite 850
1 Sansome Street
T 415 617 1300
www.britainusa.com/sf

### MONEY
**American Express**
455 Market Street
T 415 536 2600
travel.americanexpress.com

### POSTAL SERVICES
**Post Office**
4304 18th Street
T 415 431 2701
**Shipping**
UPS
T 415 775 6644
www.ups.com

### BOOKS
**San Francisco City on Golden Hills**
by Herb Caen and Dong Kingman
(Doubleday)
**This is San Francisco** by Miroslav Sasek
(Universe)
**A Crack in the Edge of the World: The
Great American Earthquake of 1906**
by Simon Winchester (Penguin Books)

### WEBSITES
**Art/Design**
www.sfarts.org
**Newspaper**
www.sfgate.com

### COST OF LIVING
**Taxi from SFO Airport to city centre**
€28
**Cappuccino**
€1.20
**Packet of cigarettes**
€3.10
**Daily newspaper**
€0.40
**Bottle of champagne**
€47

**SAN FRANCISCO**
**Area**
125 sq km
**Population**
740,000
**Currency: US Dollar**
$1 = £0.52 = €0.78
**Telephone codes**
USA: 1
San Francisco: 415
**Time**
GMT -8

CALIFORNIA

Chicago ○

□ San Francisco

○ Los Angeles

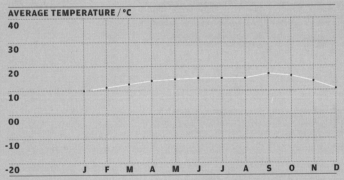

**AVERAGE TEMPERATURE / °C**

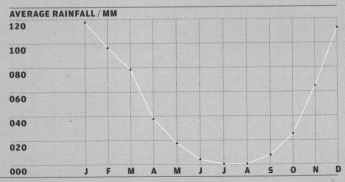

**AVERAGE RAINFALL / MM**

# NEIGHBOURHOODS
## THE AREAS YOU NEED TO KNOW AND WHY

To help you navigate the city, we've chosen the most interesting districts (see the map inside the back cover) and underlined featured venues in colour, according to their location (see below); those venues that are outside these areas are not coloured.

### NORTH BEACH
Home to countless restaurants and bars, North Beach and Telegraph Hill are in the city's north-east tip, where the hilltop art deco Coit Tower (see p010) keeps a beady eye on proceedings. Most theatres and comedy venues are to be found here.

### NOB HILL
This is where the gold and silver barons flocked in the 1800s, to be above the hoi polloi. The hill looks over the Financial District, Russian Hill and the Bay, and is home to The Fairmont hotel (see p028) and Grace Cathedral (1100 California Street, T 415 749 6300).

### HAIGHT-ASHBURY
Surely the most famous cross street in the US, Haight-Ashbury is now a sad pastiche, with relics from its psychedelic heyday and tie-dyed teens searching for ghosts of the beatniks and Grateful Dead. A few stores have tried to reinvent the area, but it's best remembered for what it once stood for, not what it has become.

### SOMA
South of Market, or SoMa, is the city's cultural epicentre, with the SF Museum of Modern Art (see p036), Museum of the African Diaspora (685 Mission Street, T 415 358 7200) and Yerba Buena Center for the Arts (701 Mission Street, T 415 978 2787) in the east, as well as the new Federal Building (see p014) and some great hotels.

### CHINATOWN
It may be home to the largest Chinese community in America, but the area is fairly contained and fascinating to explore. With China's growth as a world power, the city's geography and large Asian population give it the potential to be a major US hub.

### THE CASTRO
The heart of the west coast's gay scene, The Castro seems too outré to be true. But this is the most liberal neighbourhood in America's most liberal city, so leave your prejudices at the door and enjoy the show. Unsurprisingly, it's home to some of the best clubs and bars, and with tolerance and friendliness seemingly mandatory, whether it's your scene or not, do explore a little.

### THE MISSION
Arguably the most creative and dynamic district, the city's hottest artists, hippest bars and edgiest boutiques are all here, plus great restaurants, such as Foreign Cinema (2534 Mission Street, T 415 648 7600). The area is named after The Mission Dolores, the first Spanish settlement in the city, and the Latino community remains strong.

### HAYES VALLEY
Located between the Civic Center to the east and Alamo Square to the west, Hayes Street is the main drag and where the city's most innovative shops are located, such as Nida (see p084) and Zonal (see p076). The chains, mercifully, have been kept at bay.

# LANDMARKS

## THE SHAPE OF THE CITY SKYLINE

San Francisco is something of a landmark itself, for everything it suggests and personifies about the American psyche. Imbued with cool and charm as it is, when viewed from either the Bay or the monumental Golden Gate Bridge (see p012) as the Californian sun illuminates the buildings, it's truly a sight to behold. Then, upon entering the city and driving up and down its rollercoaster streets, it's easy to understand why Steve McQueen's Frank Bullitt was surely the coolest cop ever to appear on screen.

Hemmed in on three sides by water, as the city prospered the only way to grow was up, so the quirky splendour of the 19th-century buildings that survived the calamitous 1906 earthquake (most of the city was destroyed by the time the ensuing fires were extinguished) has since been swallowed up by the skyscrapers of downtown, many of which are bland and formulaic. The gleaming, quartz-fronted Transamerica Pyramid (see p013) by William L Pereira stands out from the crowd. It can be seen from most parts of the city and acts as a useful orientation point.

This city has its share of quirky landmarks too – for instance, Lombard Street (see p034), which draws coachloads of tourists to wonder at its sine-wave windiness, or the Dutch Windmill in Ocean Beach (Golden Gate National Recreation Area), which is a lesser known landmark internationally, but beloved by locals.
*For full addresses, see Resources.*

## Coit Tower

The 61m art deco Coit Tower stands on top of Telegraph Hill in Pioneer Park. Built using funds left to the city by a wealthy financier's widow, Lillie Hitchcock Coit, it was finished in 1933. Inside there are murals themed around the Great Depression, realised by local artists. The views of the Bay from the rotunda at the top are some of the finest in the city.
*1 Telegraph Hill Boulevard, T 415 362 0808*

### Golden Gate Bridge

One of the world's great architectural icons and instantly recognisable, the bridge's power remains undiminished when seen first-hand. The 2.7km structure spans the Pacific Ocean as it meets San Francisco Bay, its two giant towers rising more than 213m above the water. Originally intended to be painted black with yellow stripes, the bridge's guiding architect, Irving F Morrow, insisted on the now-irreplaceable International Orange. The bridge seems to accentuate its own myth, as it is frequently shrouded in mysterious fog rolling in off the ocean, or bathed in dappled California sunshine. Driving across it in a convertible is surely on everyone's must-do list.
*T 415 921 5858, www.goldengate.org*

### Transamerica Pyramid

William L Pereira's 48-floor pyramid, which was completed in 1972, dominates the Financial District and beyond, and is a useful pointer for getting your bearings in the city. Nicknamed Pereira's Prick by its detractors, it faced fierce opposition during its planning and construction, but is now as identifiable with San Francisco as the Golden Gate Bridge. The building is covered in crushed quartz, which gives it a white appearance, and viewed from over the Bay on a sunny day, it does seem to glow. After the 9/11 attacks, an observation deck near the top was closed, but large screens in the lobby display views from cameras mounted at the top of the spire. *600 Montgomery Street, T 415 983 4100, www.transamerica.com*

**Federal Building**
Still under construction at the time of
writing, this soaring new federal HQ
by architects Morphosis, who recently
completed the hulking, brutalist Caltrans
District 7 HQ in downtown LA, towers
over the SoMa district. The most radical
build in the heart of the city for decades,
it has already divided locals as to
whether it is an icon or an eyesore.
*1000 Mission Street/7th Street*

# HOTELS

## WHERE TO STAY AND WHICH ROOMS TO BOOK

For all the city's liberal leanings, its hotels remain a conservative bunch, and despite recent high-end additions, such as the St Regis (see p022), there is nothing to rival the daring concepts of the Petit Moulin in Paris or Madrid's Hotel Puerta América. That said, with classics such as the InterContinental Mark Hopkins (see p020) and The Fairmont (see p028) in town, perhaps hoteliers here don't feel the need to deviate from the hundred-year-old formula.

Nearly all the city's better hotels are to be found on the east side of town, from the vast, splendid old mansion blocks of Nob Hill to the business-and-conference chains along Market Street and The Embarcadero, and the modernist elegance of the newer builds in the SoMa district. The Orchard Garden Hotel (466 Bush Street, T 415 399 9807), the city's first 'all green' hotel, opened in 2006. Designed by Architecture International, it was built from the ground up to conform to US Green Building Council guidelines, although this in no way compromises the level of luxury guests should expect from a destination hotel in the city.

However, as both The Mission district and Potrero Hill continue to be gentrified, enticing entrepreneurs and investment, it's surely only a matter of time before a forward-thinking hotelier seizes the initiative and opens a boutique establishment or two in one of these up-and-coming areas.

*For full addresses and room rates, see Resources.*

**Phoenix Hotel**

This self-styled rock'n'roll hotel in the Tenderloin neighbourhood makes no pretence to being the swankiest in town, so if you're on business or looking for a romantic hideaway, think again. However, if you like a party and are looking to stay in a more edgy part of the city, the Phoenix is for you. Although the rooms tend to feel more motel than hotel, guests have included the Red Hot Chili Peppers and Keanu Reeves, so it has a certain cachet. To really feel like a celeb, we recommend checking into the Headliner Suite (above), while the Bambuddha Lounge (T 415 885 5088) packs in a wild crowd most nights. Enjoy original works of art scattered about, a heated outdoor pool and a free (temporary) tattoo when you check in. *601 Eddy Street, T 415 776 1380, www.jdvhospitality.com/hotels*

**Clift**

The Clift's 19th-century exterior belies the fact that, inside, Starck and Schrager have gone to town in trademark fashion. Oversized furniture and dramatic throws pepper the lobby (pictured), while rooms are Starck stark but comfortable, with nice extras, such as a Nakashima sound system. The Studio rooms present the best deal.
*495 Geary Street, T 415 775 4700,*
*www.clifthotel.com*

### InterContinental Mark Hopkins

Perched on the crest of Nob Hill, and just across the street from The Fairmont (see p028), this is a legendary San Francisco hotel, built on the spot where railroad millionaire Mark Hopkins' grand mansion once stood. The building, which appeared in Alfred Hitchcock's *Vertigo*, is situated at the intersection of three trolleybus lines, so the echt sound of San Francisco is never far away. Standard rooms are large and comfortably furnished, while the Luxury Suites, such as the California (right) and Penthouse (above) are the size of a large apartment, but correspondingly expensive. As the city outside frenetically goes about its daily business, the old-world charm and serenity inside the Mark Hopkins is very appealing, especially over a cocktail or two at the Top of the Mark (see p039). *Number One Nob Hill, 999 California Street, T 415 392 3434, san-francisco.intercontinental.com*

**St Regis Hotel**
Located in the heart of the burgeoning
cultural quarter SoMa, the St Regis Hotel
boasts its own $3.5m art collection, an
award-winning restaurant, a world-class
spa (see p093) and a butler service,
setting new standards in pared-down
opulence. The higher Superior Guest
Rooms (pictured) offer postcard views.
*125 3rd Street, T 415 284 4000,
www.stregis.com*

### Hotel Palomar

This upscale boutique hotel in downtown
San Francisco is the sassier sister of the
nearby Hotel Monaco (T 415 292 0100)
and Triton Hotel (T 415 394 0500),
and occupies the top five floors of
a refurbished 1907 landmark building.
Its rooms, such as the Executive King
(above), and lobby (right) are furnished
with contemporary glassware and
ceramics, and there is an almost op art
parquet floor, which plays havoc with
your vision if you've had one too many
margaritas. Beware also, some rooms
here are on the small side. The corner
ones overlooking Market Street are
among the more spacious. Surrealists
should stay in the René Magritte Suite,
which boasts a ceiling painted with little
fluffy clouds, and there's even a bowler
hat placed on your pillow.
*12 4th Street, T 415 348 1111,*
*www.hotelpalomar.com*

### Hotel Vitale

Opened in 2005, the Vitale is a 200-room luxury venture located at the eastern end of Mission Street, on the waterfront directly opposite the Ferry Building. Accommodation ranges from Deluxe City View or Superior Water View rooms to the Circular Suite (above) and the 67 sq m Penthouse Landmark View Suite, with its large private terrace overlooking the Bay. Most of the rooms are bright and flooded with sunlight, and the décor is minimalist but chic, such as in the lobby (right). The hotel seems geared towards helping guests relax in a serene environment: there are free yoga classes and rooftop tubs, where you can soak away the stresses of the day. There's also an excellent bar/restaurant, Americano (see p044), which gets packed at weekends, making the Vitale a welcome addition to the city.
*8 Mission Street, T 415 278 3700,*
*www.hotelvitale.com*

### The Fairmont

Completed in 1906 and scheduled to open just days before the great 'quake hit, The Fairmont (which survived largely intact thanks to its Corinthian marble columns) has remained the city's most prestigious hotel. Following an $85m restoration in 1999, the opulence and beaux arts vision of original architect Julia Morgan has been beautifully restored, while the hotel has been brought firmly into the 21st century with all the amenities you would expect. The Penthouse Suite (living room, above), the residence of choice for visiting presidents, is something else again, with its Moroccan tiling, private pool room, wood-panelled library, state dining room and breathtaking views across the Bay towards Alcatraz.

*950 Mason Street, T 415 772 5000,*
*www.fairmont.com/sanfrancisco*

### The Palace Hotel

One of the oldest and most beautiful hotels in the city, The Palace, like The Fairmont (opposite), weathered the great 'quake of 1906, and thanks to some serious renovation, it looks as splendid now as it did when it first opened in 1875. Even if you're not a guest here, the spectacular 80,000-pane stained-glass atrium of the Garden Court (overleaf), all chandeliers and marble columns, is a must-see. There are 552 rooms, such as the Deluxe Double Guest Room (above), including 34 suites, and although they don't quite match the grandeur of the atrium, they do boast four-posters, plush fabrics and tasteful art. Also worth a visit in this epitome of old-world San Francisco elegance is the Pied Piper Bar with its vast Maxfield Parrish mural. *2 New Montgomery Street, T 415 512 1111, www.sfpalace.com*

Garden Court, The Palace Hotel

# 24 HOURS

## SEE THE BEST OF THE CITY IN JUST ONE DAY

San Francisco may be a diverse place, but unlike many cities, its relatively small size makes it manageable. You can cross it by car in around 30 minutes, so don't be afraid to venture out of the neighbourhood you're staying in and explore. The public transport system here is pretty efficient, with the old trams and trolleybuses offering a historic way to traverse the city alongside the more modern buses. Few cities have the luxury of being perched on a bay, so if it's not blowing up a squall, try to take in the views from the water as well as the land.

Start the day with French toast and berries at Café de la Presse (opposite), before heading out to view the sights. The corkscrew Lombard Street (overleaf) is fun to drive down on your way to Fisherman's Wharf, where the ferries to Alcatraz (see po35) depart. The rock in the Bay is a tourist mecca, but it is a fascinating place to visit, not least for the view back to the city. The San Francisco Museum of Modern Art (see po36) is an essential stop, for the building itself as much as for the art collection.

After such a busy day, the perfect way to relax is to watch the sun set over the Pacific – and the bar at the Cliff House (see po38) is surely one of the most stunning places to see it from. End the day at the Top of the Mark (see po39), a San Francisco institution looking over the city, with a top-notch martini in hand.
*For full addresses, see Resources.*

### 08.30 Café de la Presse

Rise early and head to Café de la Presse, where the cosmopolitan feel of the city is apparent. It's situated right across from the French Consulate General, and your fellow customers are likely to be found perusing the pages of anything from Houellebecq to *Le Monde*. This is a place to be seen at as much as to watch the world go by, and breakfasts here are something of an institution. Refurbished in 2005, Café de la Presse has retained an old-world charm, but the kitchen has raised its game. Treats such as vanilla French toast with warm berries or perfect eggs Benedict with smoked salmon will set you up nicely for the day ahead.
*352 Grant Avenue, T 415 398 2680, www.cafedelapresse.com*

### 10.00 Lombard Street

Ten minutes' drive to the north-west is the infamous Lombard Street (which is one-way at this point, from west to east). Twist your way down the 'crookedest street in the United States', because you have to do it at least once. Lombard's snake-like shape was created in 1922, at the suggestion of San Francisco resident Carl Henry, to tackle the hill's natural 27-degree slope, which presented big problems for vehicles and pedestrians used to more manageable 16-degree inclines. If you don't actually drive down, the best view is from Leavenworth Street at the bottom, looking up.

### 10.30 Alcatraz

Next head to Fisherman's Wharf, before it starts heaving with tourists, and board a ferry to Alcatraz – it's wise to reserve in advance as they can get booked up, especially in peak season. The tours of the legendary prison complex in the Bay offer moving audio accounts of prisoners' lives there, and once on the island, you understand how impossible escape was, with jagged cliffs and icy, shark-infested waters awaiting anyone cunning enough to have fled their cell. The views alone, looking back towards the city from The Rock, merit the trip.
*Alcatraz Cruises, Pier 33, Hornblower Alcatraz Landing, T 415 981 7625, www.alcatrazcruises.com*

### 13.30 SF Museum of Modern Art

Once back on dry land, head to the San Francisco Museum of Modern Art in the SoMa neighbourhood, a distinctive black and white central cylinder dividing its red-brick body. Mario Botta's 1995 building still stands proud as a bold homage to art, if now somewhat dwarfed by the newer structures surrounding it. Approach it from the Yerba Buena Gardens opposite, to see the building at its very best. The museum lies on an east-west axis and sunlight floods through its circular skylight. Inside, as you'd expect, the galleries house a world-class collection, with carefully curated overviews and retrospectives. After taking in all the art, refuel with a late lunch at Caffè Museo (closed Wednesdays, T 415 357 4500). *151 3rd Street, T 415 357 4000, www.sfmoma.org*

### 17.00 Cliff House

The late afternoon sunlight on a clear day in California is unparalleled, and one of the best places to enjoy it is across town, over a long cocktail at the Cliff House. Located on the western tip of Ocean Beach with panoramic Pacific views, the Cliff House is currently in its third incarnation – the original was built on this site in 1863. It was acquired by millionaire philanthropist (and later mayor of San Francisco) Adolph Sutro in 1881, and he built a grandiose eight-storey French-style chateau. Despite surviving the great 'quake, it was destroyed by fire the following year. Sutro's daughter, Emma, oversaw the construction of the current building in 1909, which although not as grand as its predecessor, is still impressive.
*1090 Point Lobos, T 415 386 3330, www.cliffhouse.com*

### 20.00 Top of the Mark

Watch the twinkling lights come on all over town from the Top of the Mark on the 19th floor at the InterContinental Mark Hopkins (see p020). Choose from 100 different martinis and, if your feet aren't aching too much, dance to the in-house trad jazz band. During WWII, it was customary for servicemen on their way to the Pacific to have a farewell drink here with their sweethearts. They would raise a toast to the Golden Gate Bridge (see p012), believing it was blessed with good luck and would see them safely home.
*Number One Nob Hill, 999 California Street, T 415 616 6916, www.topofthemark.com*

# URBAN LIFE

## CAFÉS, RESTAURANTS, BARS AND NIGHTCLUBS

The oceanside location and the verdant land outside the city mean that chefs in San Francisco are blessed with some of the best raw ingredients in the United States, and the locals pride themselves on having a seemingly endless selection of excellent restaurants to choose from, where seafood is invariably the star of the show. Couple this with the (admittedly sometimes tedious) reverence with which wine is viewed here, and the abundance of good bottles that are produced, along with a resurgence in micro-breweries, and it means that, whether it's an eight-course blow-out, a Scooby snack or a just a quiet drink you're after, you'll be spoilt for choice. Reservations are de rigueur at most of the city's better restaurants but, curiously, even if you have booked, be prepared to kill time at the bar on arrival, because being seated at your table at the time you've arranged is a rare occurrence.

San Francisco boasts many great bars. Some of them take a bit of seeking out, but idiosyncratic venues, such as 111 Minna Gallery in the SoMa district (111 Minna Street, T 415 974 1719), are well worth the effort. The club scene is not immediately obvious either, or as open as in cities such as London or New York, but there are plenty of eclectic and interesting nights to be found. Follow our lead and, whether you're a dancing queen or a lounge lover, rest assured there's something in this city that will scratch your itch. *For full addresses, see Resources.*

**Bimbo's 365 Club**

Founded by an Italian immigrant in 1931, Bimbo's 365 was the perfect panacea for the Depression-era blues, and lines of chorus girls, including a young Rita Hayworth, high-kicked their way across the stage, much to the delight of the city's inhabitants. With its huge curving wooden bar, seductively lit lounge and spacious main room with a chequered floor and intimate circular tables (overleaf), Bimbo's provides classic, old-school supper-club entertainment, as well as hosting current crooners and artists, in a delightful art deco setting. This gem of a joint harks back to the days of big bands, broads and dames. *1025 Columbus Avenue, T 415 474 0365, www.bimbos365club.com*

Main room, Bimbo's 365

**Americano**
Chef Paul Arenstam's chic, light-filled
restaurant, with artwork framed on the
ceiling, is housed in the Hotel Vitale (see
p026). Americano does contemporary
Californian and Italian cooking to a tee.
Flaky crusted pizzas are a speciality, but
it's the ice-cream sandwich that steals
the show – we won't spoil the surprise.
*8 Mission Street, T 415 278 3777,*
*www.hotelvitale.com*

### Eddie Rickenbacker's

An amazing array of vintage motorbikes, such as Indians, Nortons, Harleys and more (one of which was presented to Clark Gable by Samuel Goldwyn for his outstanding work in *Gone with the Wind*) hang from the ceiling and adorn the walls in Eddie Rickenbacker's. Meanwhile, miniature steam trains and a veritable arsenal of rifles jostle for position with faux Lalique lamps in this one-of-a-kind bar and restaurant. A healthy selection of draught beers, whiskies and bourbons ease the uncomfortable feeling that a motorbike may be about to fall on your head.
*133 2nd Street, T 415 543 3498*

### The Blue Plate

Take a cab to this out-of-the-way location, situated at the Bernal Heights end of The Mission district, for an intimate, informal but delicious dining experience, which manages to be both down-at-home and sophisticated. There's a cramped bar for hurried diners at the front and a raised room at the rear, but it's the magical garden tucked away at the back that is the star of the show during the summer.

Tables are dotted about in a cultivated wilderness, and if you're lucky enough to bag one, the expertly cooked dishes and well-chosen wine list will ensure a dreamy meal (from 6pm, closed Sundays). *3218 Mission Street, T 415 282 6777, www.blueplatesf.com*

### Restaurant Gary Danko

It's still the hottest restaurant in town, so it's essential to book well in advance to secure a table at Gary Danko, in the rather unlikely tourist-filled Fisherman's Wharf district. Once you're through the door, it seems a world away, with the exquisite service and wow-factor food justifying Danko's celebrity. The menu is constantly modified, but signature dishes, such as glazed oysters with osetra caviar and horseradish-crusted medallions of salmon, are outstanding, as is the legendary Grand Marnier soufflé. This standard of cooking doesn't come cheap, and there are few wines below $70 a bottle, but the prices do reflect the quality and imagination on show at one of the finest restaurants on the West Coast.
*800 North Point Street/Hyde Street,*
*T 415 749 2060, www.garydanko.com*

### The Tonga Room & Hurricane Bar

If a huge tiki bar complete with rocks, indoor thunderstorms and rain showers is what you're after, the beyond-kitsch Tonga Room & Hurricane Bar at The Fairmont hotel (see p028) is the place to head. As the house band plays on a thatched boat, which floats on an indoor lagoon, the punchy Hawaiian-themed cocktails become ever more appealing. Like *Fantasy Island* come to life, this theme bar has been making punters smile and dance since the 1950s. Arrive before 7pm to take advantage of happy hour and get lost in a world of mai tai madness.
*950 Mason Street, T 415 772 5278,*
*www.fairmont.com/sanfrancisco*

## Quince

There's an intimacy and a knowing buzz at Quince, housed in an old apothecary in Pacific Heights, and the daily changing menu constantly delights those lucky enough to get a table. The décor, with its Venetian chandeliers and heavy cream napery, coupled with knowledgeable, pleasant waiting staff, give this small room a charming atmosphere. The chef and co-owner Michael Tusk sources the freshest seasonal ingredients every day and tailors his menu accordingly, which includes great dishes such as Monterey Bay squid filled with artichoke, potato and Taggiasche olives, and Laughing Stock pork loin in a wild nettle crust.
*1701 Octavia Street, T 415 775 8500, www.quincerestaurant.com*

## Carnelian Room

Upscale Californian cuisine is delivered with panache while you enjoy one of the best views in town, atop the Bank of America building. For a truly intimate meal, book the Tamalpais Room, which has a 'call button' so you can dictate the pace. Sunday brunch (10am-2.30pm, $40) is a more informal affair.
*52nd floor, 555 California Street, T 415 433 7500, www.carnelianroom.com*

### Farallon

The main room, with its suspended sculptural jellyfish, borders on the Disney-esque but the private 'caviar' rooms feel more impressive, especially the Beluga Room (pictured), with its huge undersea murals. The fantasy décor belies a serious commitment to the freshest seafood and shellfish. *450 Post Street, T 415 956 6969, www.farallonrestaurant.com*

## Limón

Look beyond the rather loud orange and lime interior at this contemporary, family-owned Peruvian restaurant near The Mission district and you'll be more than pleasantly surprised. Relaxed and friendly waiters deal with a huge amount of covers (the place is frantic at the weekend) and the chefs manage to keep the signature ceviche, in a piquant lime sauce, coming for hip and hungry diners. The *pargo rojo* (crispy whole red snapper) is a favourite too – its stunning presentation, served on a mound of coconut rice, is a conversation piece in itself. A word of warning: it appears the bathrooms were overlooked when the restaurant was renovated – a great shame. *524 Valencia Street, T 415 252 0918, www.limon-sf.com*

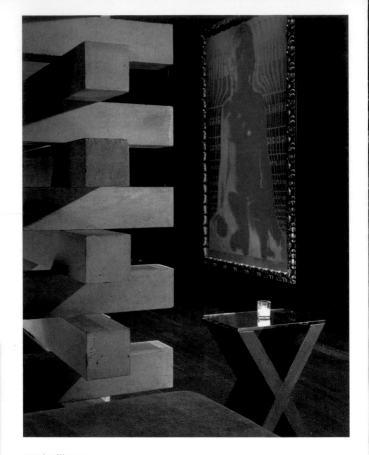

### Matrix Fillmore

Jefferson Airplane played on the opening night of the original Matrix back in 1965, and for seven years, until its closure, this venue played host to the psychedelic scene's standout bands. Reopened and reinvented in 2001, this sleek, dark club boasts a huge Jenga-like fireplace and tables spelling out 's-e-x'. A mirrored back room makes you feel rather like you're inside a limo, and some of the patrons seem to be convinced they are actually Jay-Z or Pharrell, but after a few spice-tea mojitos, you really won't mind too much.
*3138 Fillmore Street, T 415 563 4180*

## Boulevard

Housed in the historic Audiffried Building, which survived the great 'quake of 1906, Boulevard is a waterfront restaurant with views of the Bay Bridge. It has a long bar (above), an open kitchen and a grand, belle epoque feel. Since it opened in 1993, the restaurant has often been hailed as one of the best in the city, and both the setting and the cooking don't disappoint. The main room is normally bustling, while the waterfront side is quieter and more romantic. Fresh seafood is deftly handled, innovative combinations pack a punch and desserts are made in house and worth saving room for. The clued-up waiting staff always get it just right.
*1 Mission Street, T 415 543 6084,*
*www.boulevardrestaurant.com*

**Redwood Room**

Located in the Clift hotel (see p018), this is one of the most impressive-looking bars in the city. The redwood panels and skilled marquetry that line the room are unmissable, and the beautiful staff more than hold their own. Service tends towards the leisurely, so go on a quiet night to avoid the queues.
*495 Geary Street, T 415 929 2372, www.clifthotel.com*

# INSIDER'S GUIDE

## TAUBA AUERBACH, ARTIST

Tauba Auerbach is part of the high-profile Bay Area arts scene. Her work explores lettering, signage and the alphabet. As well as being exhibited at the Jack Hanley Gallery (see p082) in San Francisco, she is shown by Jeffrey Deitch in New York.

Auerbach likes to breakfast on the beautiful patio at Le Metro Café (311 Divasadero Street, T 415 552 0903). In the afternoons, she will often visit Tartine Bakery (600 Guerrero Street, T 415 487 2600) for coffee and pastries, while she thinks the Conservatory of Flowers (JFK Drive, T 415 666 7001) in Golden Gate Park makes a lovely escape. Favourite dining spots are Millennium at the Hotel California (580 Geary Street, T 415 345 3900), for the high-end vegan dishes, or Greens Restaurant (Building A, Fort Mason Center, T 415 771 6222) for its Bridge views and organic dishes.

Her recommended stores include Painted Bird (1201a Guerrero Street, T 415 401 7027), for vintage clothing and second-hand finds; Needles & Pens (3253 16th Street, T 415 255 1534), which carries art, books and T-shirts by local artists; and the cool Mollusk Surf Shop (4500 Irving Street, T 415 564 6300). After dark, Auerbach's haunts include Little Baobab (3388 19th Street, T 415 643 3558), for its Senegalese food and tamarind margaritas, and the Homestead bar (2301 Folsom Street, T 415 282 4663), which boasts pressed-tin ceilings, gold wallpaper, a wooden interior and a pot-bellied stove. *For full addresses, see Resources.*

# ARCHITOUR
## A GUIDE TO THE CITY'S ICONIC BUILDINGS

Despite some remarkable, iconic buildings completed from the mid to late 20th century, San Francisco has been conservative when it comes to architecture during the last few decades. Yes, there are a few interesting variations on the standard skyscraper but, save for the Transamerica Pyramid (see p013) and Skidmore Owings & Merrill's Alcoa Building (1 Maritime Plaza), finished back in 1967, not much stands up to scrutiny.

Rem Koolhaas gave up trying to get his Prada store concept approved in Union Square, and it was only with the triumph of Herzog & de Meuron's de Young (overleaf) that the planners have started to realise the city won't suffer from allowing some more adventurous architecture. Ricardo Legorreta's new Mission Bay campus building (1675 Owens Street) at the University of California, San Francisco, is constructed in his trademark magenta, but its relatively out-of-the-way location means it hasn't faced too much critical attention. His next project, The Mexican Museum, which will be located across the block from the San Francisco Museum of Modern Art (see p036), is eagerly awaited, as provocative museum design with a 'name' attached has become something of a global contest nowadays. The towering new Federal Building (see p014), by Morphosis, is San Francisco's bravest gamble yet, and looks set to pave the way for the city in the 21st century. *For full addresses, see Resources.*

**City Hall**

While the city has its share of dynamic and forward-thinking buildings, it also contains some stunning examples of classical architecture. City Hall, with its recently re-gilded cupola, is one of the most impressive, and the vast main hall and grand staircase are well worth a visit. There are daily guided tours, but in this most laid-back of cities, you are also free to wander the building, exploring the corridors and vast light-filled balconies. If you're lucky, you'll even see the mayor, whose grand offices are located here. Neighbouring buildings, such as the War Memorial Opera House (T 415 864 3330), Louise M Davies Symphony Hall (T 415 864 6000) and the Public Library (T 415 557 4400), form the rest of the Civic Center.
*1 Dr Carlton B Goodlett Place,*
*T 415 554 4933*

## De Young

The new-look de Young is one of Herzog
& de Meuron's most thoughtful projects.
The building is covered in perforated
and textured copper, which replicates
the impression of light filtering through
trees. As the exterior ages and acquires
its own patina, it will increasingly blend
in with the park surroundings.
*50 Hagiwara Tea Garden Drive, Golden
Gate Park, T 415 863 3330*

### Hyatt Regency

From its rather mundane entrance on The Embarcadero, you would never guess at the modernist masterpiece within – one of John Portman's boldest statements. Two floors up from street level, you emerge into a stunning concrete atrium, rising skyward and appearing to fold in on itself, with foliage dripping from the balconies above as they recede into the distance. The atrium is dominated by Charles O Perry's huge spherical anodised aluminium sculpture, *Eclipse* (1973), which sits in a black pool of water and enhances the retro sci-fi feel of the whole place. Outside, on the Bay side, there's a large, twisting, rectangular fountain, which reveals walkways and gantries that take you into the heart of the spouting water. *5 The Embarcadero Center, T 415 788 1234, www.sanfranciscoregency.hyatt.com*

### California Masonic Memorial Temple

As you would expect from men of craft in the Freemasons' Guild, the architecture of their major temples is always brave and bold, and the California headquarters is no exception. The stark, modernist, white Vermont marble exterior is striking enough, with its echoes of Mies van der Rohe and Philip Johnson, but it is the vast stained-glass window in the lobby that is the real stunner. Completed in 1957 by Emile Norman, using the endomosaic process – fabricated using parchment, metal, natural foliage, shells and even thinly sliced vegetable matter alongside the more traditional stained glass – it shows the history of Californian Masonry in charming technicolour detail. Visit towards the middle of a clear day, when the sun brings the tableau to life.
*1111 California Street*

**St Mary's Cathedral**
Architect Pietro Belluschi's cathedral is one of the Catholic Church's boldest 20th-century statements. Blessed in 1971, it has a travertine and concrete parabolic exterior, which rises from a square base to form a cross. The jaw-dropping interior emphasises this with stained-glass windows that rise up on four sides and converge at the apex. *1111 Gough Street, T 415 567 2020, www.stmarycathedralsf.org*

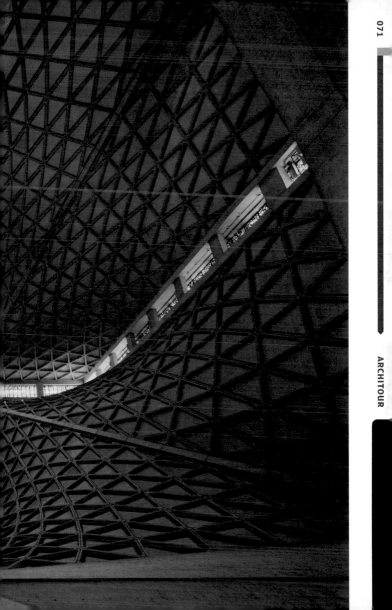

# SHOPPING

## THE BEST RETAIL THERAPY AND WHAT TO BUY

Union Square is the city's commercial centre, with department stores, such as Macy's and Neiman Marcus, located here. The surrounding streets are home to major boutiques, including Gucci, Louis Vuitton and Armani, so shopaholics can find pretty much all the name brands they could want within a few blocks.

There are some choice gourmet-food stores scattered about the city. Yum at 1750 Market Street (T 415 626 9866), where you're greeted with complimentary 'tastes' of coffee, and the legendary Molinari Delicatessen (373 Columbus Avenue, T 415 421 2337), where locals and visitors alike clamour for the authentic Italian delicacies, are two of the best. The Rainbow Grocery Cooperative (1745 Folsom Street, T 415 863 0620) is quite possibly the most politically correct grocery shop you could ever visit, and feels like something of a throwback to 1960s San Francisco.

If it's obscure music you're after, then a visit to the vast Amoeba Music at 1855 Haight Street (T 415 831 1200) is a must. Located in a former bowling alley, it's the largest independent record store in the country, and something of a mecca for visiting musicians. The City Lights Bookstore (261 Columbus Avenue, T 415 362 8193) is also a place of pilgrimage, as it was the epicentre of the beat movement on the West Coast. Lawrence Ferlinghetti still holds court, and the place is packed with radical and spiritual writings. *For full addresses, see Resources.*

#### Monument

Hollywood Regency meets Eames-era modern at Monument, which carries a good selection of larger furniture. Here, Danish sofas, beautiful credenzas and original Verner Panton pieces jostle for position with gilt-frame mirrors and Parzinger lamps. Owners Samuel Genthner and Michael de Angelis left two well-respected vintage furniture stores in the city, X-21 and Benjamin Storck respectively, to set up their own dream shop, so everything here is sourced with passion and highly desirable.
*572 Valencia Street, T 415 861 9800, www.monument.1stdibs.com*

**Paxton Gate**
From the mounted animal heads to the
raccoon penises and who knows what
else hidden in countless drawers, jars
and cabinets, you'll be amazed and
perhaps repulsed by this shop. Out
back, salvaged stained-glass windows
and architectural remnants are dotted
among the orchids in the small garden.
*824 Valencia Street, T 415 824 1872,*
*www.paxtongate.com*

### Zonal

The motto at Zonal is 'always repair, never restore', and the contents of the shop are a testament to this: worn but charming American furniture from the 1800s to the early 1900s – Hoosiers, dressers and rusting iron porch gliders – sits alongside vintage signage and American folk art. One-off objects, including a lamp crafted from an air vent, also compete for space in this packed store. Vintage items are juxtaposed with newer luxury goods, such as made-to-order furniture in soft suedes and leathers, and crisp Italian linens.
*568 Hayes Street, T 415 255 9307*

### Tradesmen

This living room-sized store is open by appointment only, with a constantly changing array of mid-century design treasures, from enormous, statement Curtis Jeré lamps to miniature but highly coveted Hagenauer figurines. Tradesmen also carries a small selection of almost impossible-to-find classic design books, such as Skurka and Gili's *Underground Interiors* from 1972. Easy to miss in the bustle of Valencia Street, but well worth investigating to see if anything catches your eye. The store seems one step ahead of the game and invariably has pieces you never knew you needed so badly.
*311 Valencia Street, T 415 552 8121*

**Past Perfect**
A trade secret for many years, this
treasure trove of vintage furniture,
antique clothes, old movie posters and
plenty more besides is heaven for prop
stylists and interior designers. The store
stretches back off Union Street and is
home to roughly 30 concessions, where
local dealers stock everything from
institutional Jean Prouvé chairs and
original Wurlitzers to antique Mexican
skulls made from amber. The vast
selection changes from week to week,
and with such a broad spread of dealers
with stalls here, if there's something
specific you're searching for, there's
a good chance they'll be able to source
it for you. The only problem you'll have
is working out how to get all those dream
purchases back home.
*2224 Union Street, T 415 929 7651*

**De Vera**

The original De Vera shop, tucked away in Maiden Lane just off bustling Union Square, is much smaller than its newer New York sibling (T 212 625 0838), but is still packed with carefully sourced *objets trouvés*, religious reliquaries and beautiful jewellery from around the world. Intricate, life-size silver stag beetles, a kaleidoscopic assemblage of mounted butterflies and moths, and delicate vintage silverware from Oaxaca are just some of the treasures to be found. The uniqueness of the items only adds to the guilty pleasure of shopping here. *29 Maiden Lane, T 415 788 0828, www.deveraobjects.com*

### Ghurka Luggage

When Marley Hodgson came across vintage leather boots and belts that once belonged to a Gurkha officer at a sale in the 1970s, it led him to develop supple, timeless leather goods that evolved into the Ghurka brand. At the store just off Union Square is a selection of some of the most exquisite, carefully crafted luggage available today. There are seasonal variations on fabrics and details with some lines, while classics such as the Kilburn and Cavalier III (above, $1,195 for the largest) weekend bags, which have been selling steadily for 30 years, remain unchanged. You may well decide to throw your existing bags away and upgrade your luggage for the trip home. *170 Post Street, T 415 392 7267, www.ghurka.com*

### Jack Hanley Gallery

Pioneer and patron of the Bay Area arts scene (see p062), Jack Hanley has two galleries, side by side on Valencia Street, which consistently show some of the most interesting artists to have emerged from San Francisco in recent years. As the loose-knit Bay Area movement has grown and achieved critical acclaim across the art world, there is little talent in the city and surrounding areas that escapes Jack's keen eye. Representing innovative artists, such as Chris Johanson, Keegan McHargue, Shaun O'Dell and Leslie Shows (whose paintings are pictured), the gallery (closed Mondays) is always worth visiting. The work is accessible and often affordable. *389 and 395 Valencia Street, T 415 522 1623, www.jackhanley.com*

### Nida

This light and airy, compact boutique
in Hayes Valley has a smart selection of
pieces, ranging from Comme des Garçons
shirts and Neil Barrett jackets for men
to the latest Luella Bartley bags, Paul &
Joe accessories and sexy Isabel Marant
dresses and tops for women. The clean,
modern space used to be a gallery, and it
shows off the eclectic selection of clothes
to full effect. Don't be dismayed that Nida
only appears to stock small sizes: this
is for display purposes only. The friendly
staff are always happy to help and
retrieve realistic sizes from the back.
*544 Hayes Street, T 415 552 4670*

### International Orange

The favourite day spa for well-groomed San Franciscans is International Orange, famed for its relaxing treatments and yoga classes. For those visiting the city on a tight schedule, when a two-hour cleanse is simply out of the question, The Shop at IO is worth a visit. Its range of exclusive products, such as the soap and lotion (above, $21 each), use organic orange oil from fruit produced on a New Mexico farm owned by one of the founders' parents. The store also sells luxe goodies by brands such as Malin+Goetz, Dr Hauschka and Aesop. In a canny move, the company was named after the trademark hue of the Golden Gate Bridge – rest assured, it's not a reference to the colour you will appear after pampering yourself with IO products. *2044 Fillmore Street, T 415 894 8811, www.internationalorange.com*

**Kozo Arts**

Sublimely patterned, intricate hand-printed Japanese papers are Kozo Arts' speciality, and there is a dazzling array of handmade books and decorative paper sheets on display. From pocket journals to personalised wedding books, any one of the many patterns and variations can be used as you require, and classes are offered on how to create these beautiful goods. But don't expect to be Kozo standard; the owners have been practising their craft for more than 14 years, and their silk-screened *chiyogami* papers are as fine as anything available in Japan.
*1969a Union Street, T 415 351 2114, www.kozoarts.com*

### Limn

For those in search of contemporary furniture and lighting, Limn, which means to draw or illuminate, is hard to beat. Initially a stockist of studio and drafting furniture for architects, the store is now housed in a 3,700 sq m former food-processing plant and offers a staggering array of products by more than 1,200 international manufacturers. Limn has done much to bring the worlds of art and design together and help break new talent. Many of the pieces it carries are unavailable elsewhere on the West Coast. *290 Townsend Street, T 415 543 5466, www.limn.com*

# SPORTS AND SPAS
## WORK OUT, CHILL OUT OR JUST WATCH

The people of San Francisco are serious about sport and fitness (though not to the near-pathological extent of Angelenos), and with the topography of the city as it is, the daily walk to work can be akin to an intense StairMaster workout. You can tell who the locals are, as they calmly stroll past the red-faced tourists huffing and puffing up the 1:3 inclines of the steeper streets. And cycle couriers here must surely give the Tour de France riders a run for their money, so, unless you're Lance Armstrong-fit, save the rental bike for crossing the Golden Gate Bridge (see p012).

With the abundance of beaches outside the city, surfing is an all-consuming passion here, although the Pacific is notoriously dangerous around San Francisco. Further south lies Santa Cruz, a mecca for surfers from across the country, and also the legendary Mavericks wave, one of the largest breaks in the world – the annual surf contest here draws the world's biggest names.

Surprisingly for a US city this size, San Francisco doesn't have an NBA franchise (you have to go over the bridge to Oakland), so baseball and American football are the sports of choice, and the concierge service at any of the better hotels should be able to procure tickets to a Giants (opposite) or 49ers (Monster Park, Jamestown Avenue/Harney Way, T 415 656 4900) home game, which are always great spectacles, even for the uninitiated.
*For full addresses, see Resources.*

### San Francisco Giants

With legends like Willie Mays and Barry Bonds having played for the San Francisco Giants, this is a city with a fine and proud baseball history. If you can score some tickets to a home game, take a trip to AT&T Park in South Beach and revel in the atmosphere. Perched on the waterfront at the southern end of The Embarcadero, the views beyond the diamond and out to San Francisco Bay make this one of the most dramatic settings for Major League baseball. If a slugger takes the plate and really connects, you might be lucky enough to see the ball go flying over the wall and into the McCovey Cove (pictured) beyond.
*AT&T Park, 24 Willie Mays Plaza,*
*T 415 972 2000, www.sfgiants.com*

**Mission Cliffs Indoor Climbing**
If the near-vertical hills in some parts
of the city aren't enough for you, this
venue has it covered, whether you're
a beginner or sherpa standard. In
case you lose your head for heights,
the recently added yoga studio and
performance cycling programme
guarantee a good workout.
*2295 Harrison Street, T 415 550 0515,*
*www.touchstoneclimbing.com*

**Ruby Sailing**

With so many tantalising views of the Bay and the Pacific to be had from the city, it's only a matter of time before you decide to don your Sperrys and succumb to the lure of the ocean. Ruby Sailing, located in China Basin, offers a two-and-a-half hour cruise ($35 per person, including lunch) with the redoubtable Captain Josh at the helm. Trips start and end beside The Ramp restaurant (T 415 621 2378), should you feel the need to steady your legs and trade tales of the high seas over a rum or two. You can either join a daily public cruise, or for $300 an hour hire the whole boat for up to 30 guests. And if things are going particularly well with a fellow passenger, the captain is even authorised to perform weddings on board.
*Departs from 855 Terry Francois Street, T 415 861 2165, www.rubysailing.com*

### Remède Spa

Serious pampering is the name of the game at the world-class Remède Spa, located in the St Regis Hotel (see p022) in SoMa. From the moment you enter, the discreet personal service and luxury robes and slippers indicate just how well you'll be looked after. Champagne, truffles, fruit and mineral water are served while you choose your treatment. Options range from the supremely good five-hour Spa Indulgence ($555, including lunch) to hot stone therapy ($190 for 90 minutes) or a customised facial ($245 for 90 minutes). Afterwards, you'll feel suitably glowing, and if you've had the paraffin foot wrap, like you're walking on air.
*St Regis Hotel, 125 3rd Street,*
*T 415 284 4060, www.stregis.com*

**Kezar Stadium**
Golden Gate Park contains many
secluded gardens and lakes, and it's
also where locals head to run off the
stresses of the day. Any number of the
drives and trails offer safe tree-lined
routes for the city's joggers, but the
truly dedicated head to Kezar Stadium's
pristine all-weather athletics track.
*Frederick Street/Stanyan Street,*
*T 415 831 6300*

# ESCAPES

## WHERE TO GO IF YOU WANT TO LEAVE TOWN

The countryside that surrounds San Francisco is some of the most beautiful America has to offer, the fault lines deep below causing a jagged, cinematic coastline and dramatic vistas. Leave the city in any direction and you will soon find yourself in epic surroundings.

A brief escape can be had by renting a bike and cycling north over the Golden Gate Bridge (see p012), either to the vista point on the far side, with its postcard views of the city (and consequent coachloads of tourists), or to the headlands beyond for more peace. If you're seeking a shady respite or a sublime connection with nature, make for Muir Woods (see p100), 19km north of Golden Gate Bridge. Although not a huge site, it's home to coast redwoods, which are among the tallest, most ancient trees on the planet, and can inspire Wordsworthian awe in the most confirmed of urbanites. One of the world's great car journeys is surely to hire a convertible and head south along the legendary Pacific Coast Highway to Carmel and Big Sur beyond, with the twisting, turning road taking you past the booming breakers of the ocean.

Heading in the other direction, north of the city, leads you to Sonoma and Napa Valley, and a dazzling array of vineyards (see p101). Thomas Keller's legendary French Laundry restaurant (6640 Washington Street, T 707 944 2380; reservations essential) can be found in nearby Yountville, for those ready to splash some cash. *For full addresses, see Resources.*

### Point Reyes National Park

There are myriad beaches and nature reserves outside San Francisco, but one of the most stunning is Point Reyes National Park. Just 50km north of the city, the landscape opens up into rolling vistas, which lead to huge beaches. Some, such as Stinson Beach, are family-oriented and suitable for swimming, whereas others, such as McClures Beach, are more dramatic, with treacherous pounding surf. The wildlife is abundant here, with pelicans, eagles and wild elk. Coastal walks, birding tours and sea kayaking trips can be arranged at Point Reyes Outdoors (T 415 663 8192). The grey whales' migratory path takes them up this coastline, and at the right time of year, from the historic Point Reyes lighthouse on the tip of the peninsula (above), you can see them clearly.

**Hearst Castle, San Simeon**
William Randolph Hearst's hilltop
compound, which he named La Cuesta
Encantada (The Enchanted Hill), is a
four-hour drive south, but a fascinating
pilgrimage. One of the largest private
houses ever built, it's unmissable for
those fascinated by displays of unbridled
wealth. Book tours in advance.
*750 Hearst Castle Road, T 805 927 2070,*
*www.hearstcastle.com*

**Muir Woods**

One of the enduring icons of California is the giant redwood, and some of the largest of these mighty trees are to be found in Muir Woods. Congressman William Kent bought the 295-acre site north of the city in 1905 to protect the woods from logging, and, in a magnanimous gesture, named the woods after conservationist John Muir, who described them as 'the best tree-lovers' monument in all the forests of the world'. In an effort to protect the more venerable examples, there is now, alas, a man-made path, but the majesty of the trees when sunlight comes flooding through is impressive all the same. Arrive as early as you can to avoid the hordes, and find yourself alone with some of the oldest living things on the planet.

*Mill Valley, T 415 388 2596,*
*www.visitmuirwoods.com*

### Wine country

Despite the mockery (and snobbery) of *Sideways*, don't be put off taking a trip into California's wine country, where some of the most interesting wines in the world today are being produced. As a sample, we suggest driving north up Highway 121 to Markham Vineyards (T 707 963 5292), one of the oldest in the valley, to sample its justly famous merlot, then heading on up to Rombauer Vineyards (T 707 963 5170), to take in the amazing views from its glass-walled tasting room. Just down the road is Duckhorn (above, T 888 354 8885), one of the most forward-thinking vineyards in Napa, with its clubhouse-style tasting room. As you head back to the city, drop in on its sister winery, Paraduxx (T 707 945 0890), for a wine-tasting menu with hors d'oeuvres pairings – a fine way to round things off.

**Monterey Bay Aquarium**
An hour's drive south of San Francisco,
this is arguably the best aquarium
in the country. Its considered, almost
nostalgic architecture, with scores of
decks overlooking the ocean, is a winner,
while the diversity of aquatic species and
engaging ways in which they are housed
will absorb keen Cousteaus of all ages.
*886 Cannery Row, T 831 648 4800,
www.mbayaq.org*

# NOTES
**SKETCHES AND MEMOS**

# RESOURCES

## CITY GUIDE DIRECTORY

**A**

**Alcatraz Cruises** 035
Pier 33
Hornblower Alcatraz Landing
T 415 981 7625
www.alcatrazcruises.com

**Alcoa Building** 064
1 Maritime Plaza

**Americano** 044
Hotel Vitale
8 Mission Street
T 415 278 3777
www.hotelvitale.com

**Amoeba Music** 072
1855 Haight Street
T 415 831 1200
www.amoebamusic.com

**B**

**Bambuddha Lounge** 017
Phoenix Hotel
601 Eddy Street
T 415 885 5088
www.bambuddhalounge.com

**Bimbo's 365 Club** 041
1025 Columbus Avenue
T 415 474 0365
www.bimbos365club.com

**The Blue Plate** 047
3218 Mission Street
T 415 282 6777
www.blueplatesf.com

**Boulevard** 059
1 Mission Street
T 415 543 6084
www.boulevardrestaurant.com

**C**

**Café de la Presse** 033
352 Grant Avenue
T 415 398 2680
www.cafedelapresse.com

**Caffè Museo** 036
San Francisco Museum of Modern Art
151 3rd Street
T 415 357 4500
www.sfmoma.org

**California Masonic
Memorial Temple** 069
1111 California Street

**Carnelian Room** 052
52nd floor
555 California Street
T 415 433 7500
www.carnelianroom.com

**City Hall** 065
1 Dr Carlton B Goodlett Place
T 415 554 4933
www.sfgov.org

**City Lights Bookstore** 072
261 Columbus Avenue
T 415 362 8193
www.citylights.com

**Cliff House** 038
1090 Point Lobos
T 415 386 3330
www.cliffhouse.com

**Coit Tower** 010
1 Telegraph Hill Boulevard
T 415 362 0808
www.coittower.org

**Conservatory of Flowers** 062
JFK Drive
Golden Gate Park
T 415 666 7001
www.conservatoryofflowers.org

# HOTELS

## ADDRESSES AND ROOM RATES

**Clift** 018
Room rates:
double, from $365;
Studio, from $465
*495 Geary Street*
*T 415 775 4700*
*www.clifthotel.com*

**The Fairmont** 028
Room rates:
double, from $340;
Penthouse Suite, $10,000
*950 Mason Street*
*T 415 772 5000*
*www.fairmont.com/sanfrancisco*

**InterContinental Mark Hopkins** 020
Room rates:
double, from $179;
Standard Room, from $179;
Luxury Suite, from $1,450
*Number One Nob Hill*
*999 California Street*
*T 415 392 3434*
*san-francisco.intercontinental.com*

**Hotel Monaco** 024
Room rates:
double, $319
*501 Geary Street*
*T 415 292 0100*
*www.monaco-sf.com*

**Orchard Garden Hotel** 016
Room rates:
prices on request
*466 Bush Street*
*T 415 399 9807*
*www.theorchardgardenhotel.com*

**The Palace Hotel** 029
Room rates:
double, $569;
Deluxe Double Guest Room, $569
*2 New Montgomery Street*
*T 415 512 1111*
*www.sfpalace.com*

**Hotel Palomar** 024
Room rates:
double, from $219;
René Magritte Suite, $969
*12 4th Street*
*T 415 348 1111*
*www.hotelpalomar.com*

**Phoenix Hotel** 017
Room rates:
double, $99-$149;
Headliner Suite, $299-$349
*601 Eddy Street*
*T 415 776 1380*
*www.jdvhospitality.com/hotels*

**St Regis Hotel** 022
Room rates:
double, from $409
Superior Guest Room, from $499
*125 3rd Street*
*T 415 284 4000*
*www.stregis.com*

**Triton Hotel** 024
 Room rates:
 double, $120-$400
 *342 Grant Avenue*
 *T 415 394 0500*
 *www.hoteltriton.com*
**Hotel Vitale** 076
 Room rates:
 double, $309;
 Deluxe City View, $339;
 Superior Water View, $369;
 Circular Suite, $699;
 Penthouse Landmark View Suite, $1,500
 *8 Mission Street*
 *T 415 278 3700*
 *www.hotelvitale.com*

## WALLPAPER* CITY GUIDES

**Editorial Director**
Richard Cook

**Art Director**
Loran Stosskopf

**City Editor**
James Reid

**Project Editor**
Rachael Moloney

**Executive Managing Editor**
Jessica Firmin

**Chief Designer**
Ben Blossom

**Designer**
Ingvild Sandal

**Map Illustrator**
Russell Bell

**Photography Editor**
James Reid

**Photography Assistant**
Jasmine Labeau

**Chief Sub-Editor**
Jeremy Case

**Sub-Editor**
Vicky McGinlay

**Assistant Sub-Editor**
Milly Nolan

**Intern**
Sylvie Subba

**Wallpaper* Group Editor-in-Chief**
Jeremy Langmead

**Creative Director**
Tony Chambers

**Publishing Director**
Fiona Dent

**Contributors**
Paul Barnes
Jeroen Bergmans
Alan Fletcher
Sara Henrichs
David McKendrick
Claudia Perin
Meirion Pritchard
Ellie Stathaki

**Thanks to**
Zack Camacho
Dan, Debra and Sarah Delaney
Scott Lincoln

## PHAIDON

**Phaidon Press Limited**
Regent's Wharf
All Saints Street
London N1 9PA

**Phaidon Press Inc**
180 Varick Street
New York, NY 10014
www.phaidon.com

First published 2007
© 2007 Phaidon
Press Limited

ISBN 978 0 7148 4730 6

A CIP Catalogue record
for this book is available
from the British Library.

All prices are correct at
time of going to press,
but are subject to change.

Printed in China

## PHOTOGRAPHERS

# SAN FRANCISCO
## A COLOUR-CODED GUIDE TO THE HOT 'HOODS

### NORTH BEACH
The north-east tip of the city boasts bars, restaurants, theatres and comedy venues

### NOB HILL
This affluent neighbourhood is the place to come for unrivalled views of the city

### HAIGHT-ASHBURY
Follow the beat or hippie trail through this district and swing by the iconic crossroads

### SOMA
A mind-broadening cultural hot spot, where you'll find many of the city's best museums

### CHINATOWN
A fast-paced, fascinating area that's home to the largest Chinese community in the US

### THE CASTRO
It's party central in the bars and restaurants of the West Coast's wildest gay scene

### THE MISSION
Cutting-edge art, hip bars and designer stores have moved into the old Spanish quarter

### HAYES VALLEY
This area's central street is a shopaholic's dream as it's lined with quirky boutiques

For a full description of each neighbourhood,
including the places you really must not miss, see the Introduction